Hunting with Rifles

Annie Wendt Hemstock

PowerKiDS press
New York

Published in 2015 by The Rosen Publishing Group, Inc.
29 East 21st Street, New York, NY 10010

First Edition

Editor: Amelie von Zumbusch
Book Design: Greg Tucker
Book Layout: Joe Carney
Photo Researcher: Katie Stryker

Photo Credits: p. 4 Christiane Bouvier Rose/Shutterstock.com; p. 5 Popperfoto/Getty Images; p. 6 Tony Campbell/Shutterstock.com; p. 7 Mary Ann McDonald/Shutterstock.com; p. 8 ppart/iStock/Thinkstock; p. 9 SteveMcsweeny/iStock/Thinkstock; p. 11 Zoran Skaljac/iStock/Thinkstock; p. 13 DreamPictures/Photolibrary/Getty Images; p. 14 Lisa Combs/iStock/Thinkstock; p. 15 monkeybusinessimages/iStock/Thinkstock; p. 17 Ana Gram/Shutterstock.com; p. 19 Joel Guay/Shodanphotos/Flickr/Getty Images; p. 20 Volodymyr Burdiak/Shutterstock.com; p. 21 Philip W. Kirkland/Shutterstock.com; p. 22 Steve Baxter/iStock/Thinkstock; p. 23 Billy Gadbury/Shutterstock.com; p. 25 Nathan Allred/iStock/Thinkstock; p. 26 Randy Hayashi/iStock/Thinkstock; p. 27 Seth Joel/Photographer's Choice RF/Getty Images; p. 29 Mighty Sequoia Studio/Shutterstock.com.

Library of Congress Cataloging-in-Publication Data

Hemstock, Annie Wendt, author.
Hunting with rifles / by Annie Wendt Hemstock. — First edition.
pages cm. — (Open season)
Includes index.
ISBN 978-1-4777-6710-8 (library binding) — ISBN 978-1-4777-6711-5 (pbk.) — ISBN 978-1-4777-6712-2 (6-pack)
1. Hunting rifles—Juvenile literature. 2. Hunting—Juvenile literature. 3. Shooting—Juvenile literature. I. Title.
SK274.2.H46 2015
799.2028'32—dc23

2014000310

Manufactured in the United States of America

CPSIA Compliance Information: Batch #WS14PK3: For Further Information contact Rosen Publishing, New York, New York at 1-800-237-9932

Contents

Get in the Groove

People have been using guns for centuries. Early guns were loaded through the end of the barrel, or muzzle. They had to be reloaded after each shot. They did not work well if the gunpowder got wet. Muzzleloaders were not very accurate.

Gunsmiths learned to put grooves inside a gun's barrel. The grooves made the gun more accurate and able to shoot farther. These grooves, called rifling, are what gave modern rifles their name.

This young hunter is practicing aiming and firing a rifle. It takes practice to do so well.

Rifles have been around for a long time. Today's rifles can shoot farther and with more accuracy than the rifle in this photo could.

Rifles use cartridges with bullets and gunpowder inside. Most rifles can hold more than one cartridge at a time. They are accurate and can shoot long distances. People have hunted with rifles since these guns were invented.

Animals that you hunt are called game. Most of the game you hunt with a rifle are **mammals**. Deer, moose, elk, and bears are big game. There are more than 20 big-game **species** in North America. In some places, it is also legal to hunt small game with rifles. Rabbits, woodchucks, coyotes, and prairie dogs are small-game animals. Some small-game animals are hunted for their meat. Others are hunted for their fur. Some small animals are called **varmints**. They are hunted without limits because they can cause problems for people.

Deer like this one are among the most popular big-game animals to hunt.

This elk is a big-game animal. Elk hunters must be good shots and have powerful rifles to hunt these large creatures.

In some areas, there are laws against hunting with rifles. Some kinds of game, like **waterfowl**, can be hunted only with a shotgun. Make sure you know the laws in your area.

Know the Parts

A rifle is a long gun that shoots a single bullet at a time. The part you hold against your shoulder is the stock. Gun stocks are made from wood or something man-made, like plastic.

The barrel is the tube that launches the bullet. The inside of a gun barrel is called the bore. The muzzle is the end where the bullet leaves the gun. The opposite end is called the breech. Some rifles have sights, while others have a scope. Both are used to aim the rifle.

A rifle is a long gun. This does not just mean that it is a gun that is long, though. A long gun is a gun that was designed to be braced against a person's shoulder when fired.

The working parts of a rifle are attached to the **receiver**. These are the parts that make the gun fire. The trigger is the lever you pull when you shoot the gun.

So Many Options

How do you know which kind of rifle to choose? Let's look at some common kinds. Some rifles will fire only one bullet before you have to reload. These are single-shot rifles. They are simple, with few moving parts. You have to make each shot count. Some hunters like the challenge of having only one shot.

Other rifles hold more than one bullet. You do not have to reload after each shot. These are called repeating rifles. Repeating rifles have **actions** that load, fire, and reload more than one shot in a row. This kind of gun may have a bolt or a lever that the hunter moves to work the action. Repeating rifles make it easier and faster to take another shot.

Hunting Facts

The rifling inside the barrel makes the bullet spin. A spinning bullet flies farther and straighter, as a spinning football does.

There are several different kinds of rifles with various actions. A hunter should try out as many rifles as possible to find the right one.

Rifles also come in many calibers. The caliber is the distance across the bore. Some calibers are measured in parts of an inch. The .22 and the .308 are examples. Other calibers are measured with the metric system, like the 7 mm.

It is important to match the rifle to your **quarry**. A small-caliber gun is used to hunt small game. A large-caliber rifle is used for big game. You want your rifle to have enough power to kill your quarry in a way that does not cause it to suffer. For example, a .22-caliber rifle is a good choice for squirrels or rabbits but not for deer. A .308 would be a better deer-hunting rifle but is too big for hunting rabbits.

Rifles come in different calibers. A clerk at a gun store can help you find the right caliber for the right game.

Round and Round We Go

Rifle ammunition is called a cartridge or a round. The outside is the brass case. Inside, there is gunpowder. On the base of the case, there is a **primer**.

The bullet fits snugly into the open end of the case. Bullets come in different calibers and shapes. The weight of a bullet is measured in grains. There are 7,000 grains in 1 pound (454 g). Most bullets are made of lead. Some are covered with metal jackets. Hunting ammunition is made to flatten out when it hits.

These cartridges are for a rifle. It is important always to use the correct cartridge for your rifle.

Hunting Facts

When you pull the trigger, a metal pin hits the primer. The primer explodes, which makes the powder burn. Gases from the burning powder push the bullet down the barrel.

You can find charts that show what ammunition is good for hunting which game online.

There are many kinds of rifle ammunition. Make sure the cartridges you pick are made for your caliber of rifle. There are charts to help you pick the best ammunition for the game you are going to hunt.

Once you get to where you will be shooting, you can load your rifle. Put the **safety** on. Make sure the **chamber** is empty and there is nothing in the barrel. Keep the barrel pointed in a safe direction.

Your rifle's action will affect how you load it. With a single-shot rifle, you load the round into the chamber and close the action. With repeating rifles, you load the cartridges into **magazines**. Work the action to move a cartridge into the chamber.

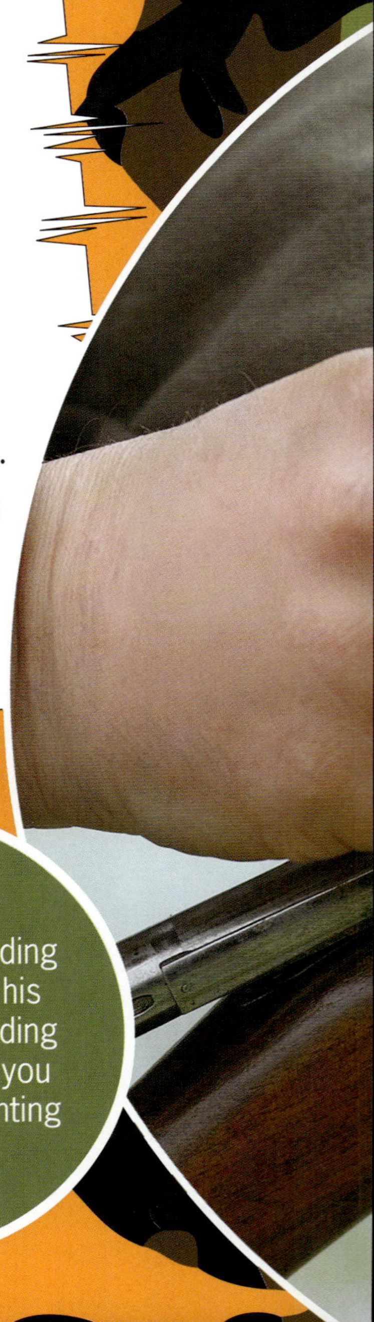

This hunter is loading a cartridge into his rifle. Practice loading your rifle before you head out on a hunting trip with it.

As you head into the field, handle your rifle safely. Keep the safety on until you are ready to shoot. The safest way to carry a rifle is with both hands. Always be aware of where your rifle is pointing.

Hunting Facts

Each rifle has markings on the barrel called a data stamp. The data stamp will tell you what kind of cartridge to use in that rifle. Using the wrong ammunition can be very dangerous.

Aim

Rifles are accurate only if you know how to aim. There is a post or bead on the muzzle end of the barrel. This is the front sight. If you have open sights on your rifle, the rear sight is a flat piece of metal with a notch or groove. If you have an aperture sight, the rear sight will be a small ring, which you look through. This is also called a peep sight.

To aim your rifle, hold the gun against your shoulder. Look down the barrel. The top of the front sight should line up with the spot where you want the bullet to hit. You should see the front sight in the middle of the notch or ring of the rear sight.

This hunter is practicing her aim at a special field called a firing range. Firing ranges are places to practice your shooting.

To make it easier to aim, some hunters mount scopes above their guns' barrels. A scope is a tube with a lens at each end that makes your target look closer. Some scopes have power rings that let you change how close the target looks.

When you look through a scope, you see two thin lines. These are called reticles or crosshairs. To aim, put the spot where the crosshairs meet on the spot that you want to hit.

Scopes can help hunters see faraway animals like this moose. The red spot at the center of the crosshairs is where the bullet will hit.

This hunter is sighting in the scope on his rifle. Sighting in a scope is the process of adjusting the sights to make sure that you can aim accurately through them.

Most scopes have two adjustment knobs. The windage knob lets you move the crosshair from side to side. The elevation knob lets you adjust up and down. By moving the knobs, you can set your scope so that the point where the crosshairs meet lines up with where your rifle shoots.

Fire!

It is very important to hold the gun steady. Hold your breath, and gently squeeze the trigger without jerking.

Your rifle is loaded and you have your target in your sights. Make sure there is nothing behind your target that could be hit if you miss. Take a deep breath, then let it out about halfway. Now, hold your breath. If you breathe while you fire, your chest will expand and your gun will move. Make sure your sights are aligned on your target and gently squeeze the trigger. If you jerk the trigger, it can cause you to miss.

Hunting Facts

The four shooting positions are prone, sitting, kneeling, and standing. "Prone" means "lying down." It is the most stable position from which to shoot. The least stable is standing.

When you fire, make sure to brace the stock against your shoulder and not your armpit.

When the shot goes off, keep aiming at your target. Count to three before you lower your rifle. This is called following through. It keeps you from moving your gun too soon, which can cause you to miss your shot.

A Good Hunter

There is a lot that goes into being a good hunter. As a good hunter, you will know the hunting laws. You will have a license if you need one. A license gives you permission to hunt legally. You will know how many animals you are allowed to take. This is called the bag limit. For some animals, like deer, you need to register your kill.

A good hunter is a safe hunter. Always treat your gun as if it were loaded. Always know who is around you. Always keep the muzzle of your gun pointed in a safe direction. Never point it at something you do not intend to shoot.

Always carry your rifle so that it is pointed away from people. Keep the safety on, and keep your fingers off the trigger until you are ready to fire.

There is so much to learn about hunting! A good place to start is by taking a hunter safety class. You may need to pass the class before you can hunt. In the class, you will learn how to shoot properly and about guns and ammunition. You learn how to be a good, safe hunter.

Practicing your shooting, as this young hunter is doing, is the best way to improve your aim.

Targets like this one are used on firing ranges. The goal is to get a tight cluster of shots as close to the center as possible.

Once you know the basics, it is time to practice. The more you shoot, the more natural and comfortable it feels. Practicing with targets will make you a better shot. You will learn how to hit where you are aiming with every shot. You will be less nervous if you feel good about your shooting skills. You will know where to aim, and you will know how to make a good, clean shot.

Carrying on the Tradition

People have used firearms for hunting since they were invented. Hunting lets us put food on our tables. It gets us outdoors and into the woods and fields. We become a part of the natural world around us.

Some of the money that hunters spend on licenses is used to make sure wildlife has a place to live. Hunting is an important part of game management. Hunters help make sure that game **populations** don't get too big.

Hunters help keep game populations at a safe number. Responsible hunters protect the habitats of game animals like this bear.

If you are interested in hunting, try to find someone to help you learn. Many hunters are willing to help others become good hunters, too. Someday, you might even help another young hunter get started in this great sport!

Happy Hunting

- Always handle a gun safely. Treat it as if it were loaded, even if you know it is empty.
- Never point a gun at something you don't intend to shoot.
- Keep your finger away from the trigger until you are ready to shoot.
- Make sure your ammunition matches the data stamp on your gun.
- Practice with the same ammunition you will use when you are hunting.
- Make sure your sights are set so you will hit where you aim. Scopes need to be set right, too.
- Learn about your quarry so you know where to aim for a good shot that will kill.
- Know and follow the hunting laws for your area.
- Keep your rifle clean and in good condition. If you find a problem, take it to a gunsmith instead of trying to fix it yourself.
- Store your gun unloaded, at home and in the field.

Glossary

actions (AK-shunz) The parts of guns that load, fire, and remove ammunition.

chamber (CHAYM-bur) The part of a gun that receives the charge.

gunsmiths (GUN-smiths) People whose trade involves the making or repairing of firearms.

magazines (MA-guh-zeenz) The parts of guns that store ammunition.

mammals (MA-mulz) Warm-blooded animals that have backbones and hair, breathe air, and feed milk to their young.

populations (pop-yoo-LAY-shunz) Groups of animals or people living in the same place.

primer (PRY-mur) Something that will catch fire and is used to set off the gunpowder.

quarry (KWOR-ee) Something that is being hunted.

receiver (rih-SEE-ver) The part of a gun that holds the parts that make it fire.

safety (SAYF-tee) A part on a gun that keeps it from being fired by mistake.

species (SPEE-sheez) Kinds of living things. All people are one species.

varmints (VAHR-munts) Animals that are considered pests and can often be hunted without a license.

waterfowl (WAH-ter-fowl) Ducks, geese, swans, and similar waterbirds.

Index

Websites

Due to the changing nature of Internet links, PowerKids Press has developed an online list of websites related to the subject of this book. This site is updated regularly. Please use this link to access the list:
www.powerkidslinks.com/os/rifle/